The Illustrated
Christmas Story

by Bob Bond

**With 21 carols,
arranged for piano and voice**

AMSCO PUBLICATIONS
part of The Music Sales Group
London / New York / Nashville / Los Angeles / Paris / Sydney / Copenhagen / Berlin / Madrid / Tokyo

Published by
Amsco Publications
257 Park Avenue South, New York, NY 10010, United States of America.

Exclusive distributors:
Music Sales Corporation
257 Park Avenue South, New York, NY 10010, United States of America.

Music Sales Limited
Distribution Centre, Newmarket Road,
Bury St Edmunds, Suffolk, IP33 3YB, England.

Music Sales Pty Limited
120 Rothschild Avenue, Rosebery, NSW 2018, Australia.

Order No. AM989450
ISBN-10: 0-8256-3550-0
ISBN-13: 978-0-8256-3550-2

Project editor: Heather Ramage.
Music arranged by Paul Honey.
Music processed by Paul Ewers Music Design.

Illustrated by Bob Bond.
Publishing concept and scenario: Ed Chatelier
Creative Agency: The Edge Group (www.edgeart.org)

Printed in Peru by Quebecor World.

www.musicsales.com

Your Guarantee of Quality:
As publishers, we strive to produce every book
to the highest commercial standards.

The music has been freshly engraved and the book
has been carefully designed to minimize awkward page turns
and to make playing from it a real pleasure.

This pulp is from farmed sustainable forests and
was produced with special regard for the environment.

Throughout, the printing and binding have been
planned to ensure a sturdy, attractive publication which
should give years of enjoyment.

If your copy fails to meet our high standards, please inform us
and we will gladly replace it.

CAROLS

At the time of Jesus' birth
Two thousand years ago,

The occasion was celebrated
Not with turkeys, trees or snow,

It was the news of the Savior's birth
That brought people from afar,
And all who came to kneel
before him
Were guided by the Christmas star,

Aaaaah!

Some men could tell the future
And the coming of God's Son.
The scripture calls them prophets,
And here is such a one…

Old Isaiah, years before,
He was the first to tell,
One day a baby would be born…

God with us
—Emmanuel!

There was more about this baby;
Here was another sign—
He'd come from Israel's chosen,
And out of David's line.

And Micah also wrote a book,
This, too, was in the plot.
The little town of Bethlehem
Was going to be the spot.

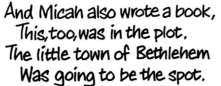

Many centuries have passed,
  And kings have come and gone;
The time is now exactly right
  For this baby to be born.

So here she is, young Mary,
  The perfect girl God's found.
This is the day to surprise her
And send an angel round.

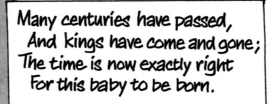

I've come to tell you, Mary,
You will give birth to a baby boy.

7

Then Mary put her cloak on,
    And to the hills she came
To where her married cousin lived,
    Elizabeth her name.

Elizabeth was old and bent
    Yet holy, meek, and mild.
She, too, had found God's favor,
    She, too, would have a child.

When Mary came in
    through the door
Elizabeth said:

My word!
My baby jumped
inside me!
Mary, praise the Lord!

And Mary raised her
    eyes to heaven:

My soul is
really blessed!
For God has looked
with favor
On me above
the rest!

What Child Is This?

Words by William Chatterton Dixon
Music: Traditional

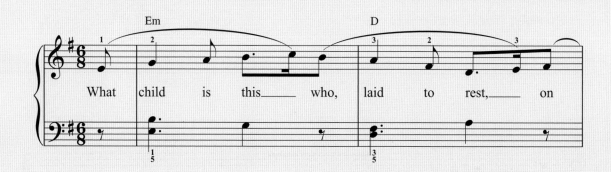

What child is this_ who, laid to rest,_ on

Mar - y's lap_ is sleep - ing? Whom an - gels greet_ with

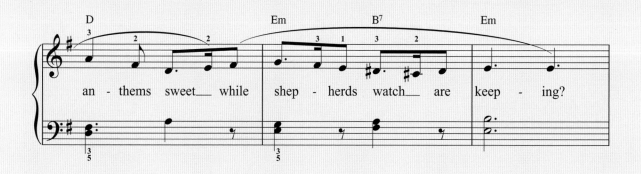

an - thems sweet_ while shep - herds watch_ are keep - ing?

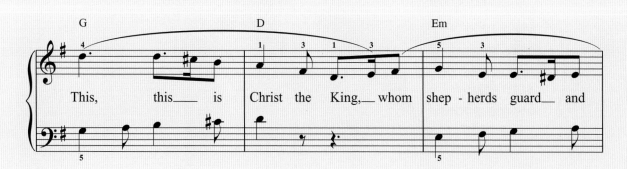

This, this_ is Christ the King,_ whom shep - herds guard_ and

an - gels sing; haste, haste to bring Him laud, the

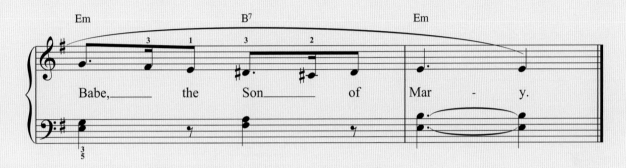

Babe, the Son of Mar - y.

2 Why lies he in such mean estate,
Where ox and ass are feeding?
Good Christians, fear; for sinners here
The silent word is pleading.

This, this...

3 So bring Him incense, gold, and myrrh,
Come peasant, king to own Him;
The King of kings, salvation brings;
Let loving hearts enthrone Him.

This, this...

Infant Holy, Infant Lowly

Traditional

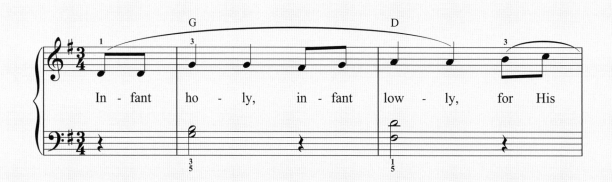

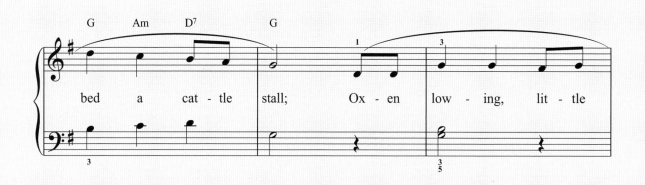

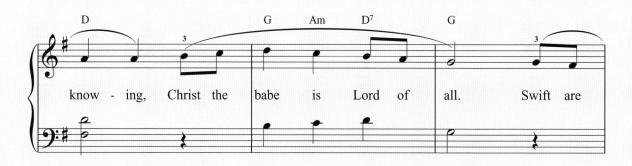

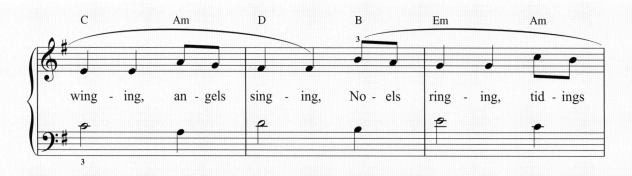

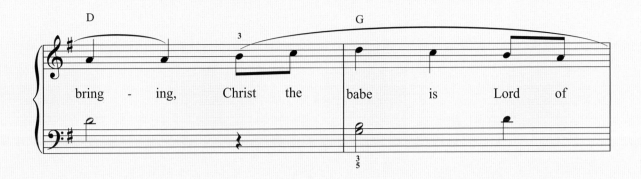

bring - ing, Christ the babe is Lord of

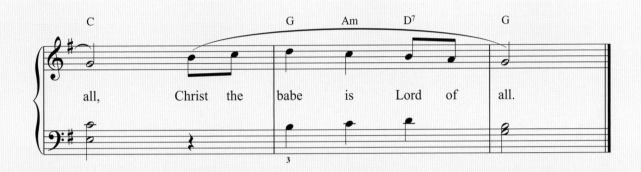

all, Christ the babe is Lord of all.

2 Flocks were sleeping, shepherds keeping
Vigil till the morning new,
Saw the glory, heard the story,
Tidings of a gospel true.
Thus rejoicing, free from sorrow,
Praises voicing, greet the morrow,
Christ the babe was born for you,
Christ the babe was born for you.

O Come, O Come, Emmanuel

Words by John Neale
Music: Traditional

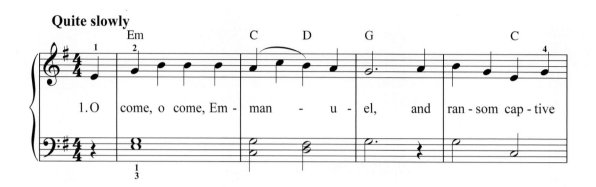

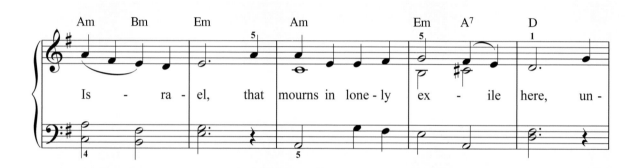

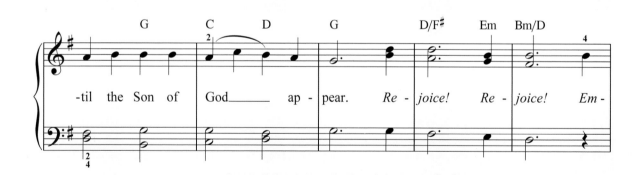

2 O come thou rod of Jesse, free
Thine own from Satan's tyranny;
From depths of hell thy people save,
And give them vict'ry o'er the grave.

Rejoice! Rejoice!...

3 O come, thou dayspring, come and cheer
Our spirits by thine advent here;
Disperse the gloomy clouds of night,
And death's dark shadows put to flight.

Rejoice! Rejoice!...

4 O come, thou key of David, come,
And open wide our heav'nly home;
Make safe the way that leads on high,
And close the path to misery.

Rejoice! Rejoice!...

5 O come, o come, thou Lord of might,
Who to thy tribes, on Sinai's height
In ancient times didst give the Law
In cloud, and majesty and awe.

Rejoice! Rejoice!...

O Holy Night

Music by A. Adam

So here's Elizabeth's little boy
  Delivered safe and sound,
To share the couple's happiness,
  The neighbors gather round.

His father, Zechariah,
  For months had been struck dumb.
He watched in silent wonder
  To see his baby come.

He should have his father's name, when all is said and done...

But dad called for a slate and chalk, And wrote:

HIS NAME IS JOHN

Soon after, Mary's time drew near, She, too, would be a mom, And she and Joseph wondered:

What will our child become?

18

The Governor decided at that time
 A census should be taken.

So here they are, to Bethlehem,
 The long trek they are making.

Joseph, Mary, donkey too,
 So weary all of them...

Until, at last, their journey's end—
The town of Bethlehem.

It's night—they need to find a bed,
But where do they begin?

No friends, no help, no sympathy,
And...

No room at the inn!

20

But one takes pity on them
And it isn't long before...

Mary has her baby boy
In a stable on the floor.

Once In Royal David's City

Words by Cecil Alexander
Music by Henry Gauntlett

Moderately slow

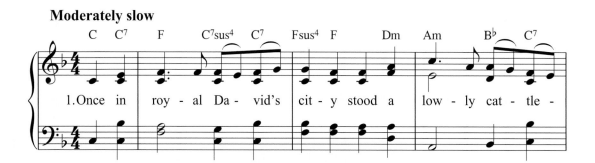

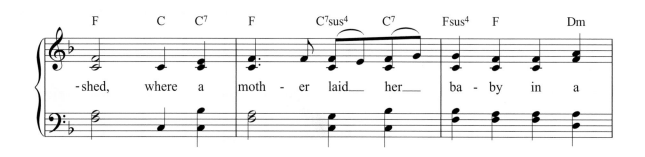

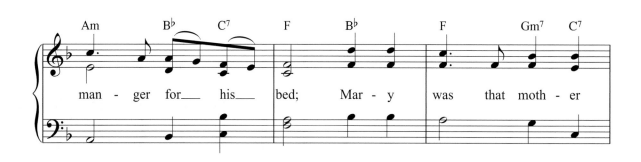

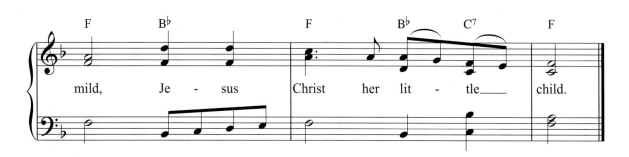

2 He came down to earth from heaven
Who is God and Lord of all,
And his shelter was a stable,
And his cradle was a stall;
With the poor and mean and lowly,
Lived on earth our Savior holy.

3 And through all his wondrous childhood
He would honor and obey,
Love and watch the lowly Maiden,
In whose gentle arms he lay:
Christian children all must be
Mild, obedient, good as he.

4 For he is our childhood's pattern,
Day by day like us he grew,
He was little, weak and helpless,
Tears and smiles like us he knew;
And he feeleth for our sadness,
And he shareth in our gladness.

5 And our eyes at last shall see him,
Through his own redeeming love,
For that child so dear and gentle
Is our Lord in heaven above;
And he leads his children on
To the place where he is gone.

6 Not in that poor lowly stable,
With the oxen standing by,
We shall see him; but in heaven,
Set at God's right hand on high;
Where like stars his children crowned
All in white shall wait around.

O Little Town Of Bethlehem

Words by Phillips Brooks
Music by Lewis Redner

all the years are met in thee to-night. 2.For - el.

2 For Christ is born of Mary;
   And, gathered all above,
   While mortals sleep, the angels keep
   Their watch of wond'ring love.
   O morning stars, together
   Proclaim the holy birth,
   And praises sing to God the King,
   And peace to men on earth!

3 How silently, how silently,
   The wondrous gift is giv'n!
   So God imparts to human hearts
   The blessings of his heav'n.
   No ear may hear his coming;
   But in this world of sin,
   Where meek souls will receive him, still
   The dear Christ enters in.

4 O holy child of Bethlehem,
   Descend to us, we pray;
   Cast out our sin, and enter in,
   Be born in us today.
   We hear the Christmas angels
   The great glad tidings tell:
   O come to us, abide with us,
   Our Lord Emmanuel.

Silent Night

Words by Joseph Mohr
Music by Franz Gruber

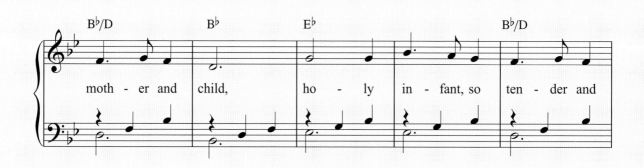

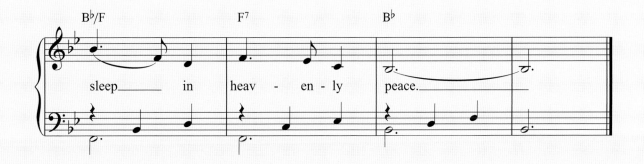

sleep_____ in heav - en - ly peace._____

2 Silent night, holy night.
Shepherds quake at the sight,
Glories stream from heaven afar,
Heav'nly hosts sing alleluia:
Christ, the Savior is born,
Christ, the Savior is born.

3 Silent night, holy night.
Son of God, love's pure light,
Radiant beams from thy holy face,
With the dawn of redeeming grace:
Jesus, Lord, at thy birth,
Jesus, Lord, at thy birth.

Away In A Manger

Words by William Kirkpatrick
Music by James R. Murray

lit - tle Lord Je - sus a - sleep in the hay.

2 The cattle are lowing, the baby awakes,
But little Lord Jesus no crying he makes.
I love thee, Lord Jesus! Look down from the sky,
And stay by my side until morning is nigh.

3 Be near me, Lord Jesus; I ask thee to stay
Close by me forever, and love me, I pray.
Bless all the dear children in thy tender care,
And fit us for heaven, to live with thee there.

While Shepherds Watched

Words by Nahum Tate
Music: Traditional

2. "Fear not," said he (for mighty dread
   Had seized their troubled mind);
   "Glad tidings of great joy I bring
   To you and all mankind."

3. "To you in David's town this day
   Is born in David's line
   A Savior, who is Christ the Lord;
   And this shall be the sign":

4. "The heav'nly babe you there shall find
   To human view displayed,
   All meanly wrapped in swathing bands,
   And in a manger laid."

5. Thus spake the seraph, and forthwith
   Appeared a shining throng
   Of angels praising God, who thus
   Addressed their joyful song:

6. "All glory be to God on high,
   And to the earth be peace;
   Good will henceforth from heav'n to men
   Begin and never cease."

It Came Upon The Midnight Clear

Words by Edmund Hamilton Sears
Music by Richard Storrs Willis

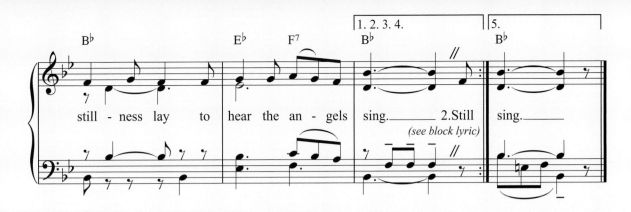

still - ness lay to hear the an - gels sing._____ 2.Still sing._____

(see block lyric)

2 Still through the cloven skies they come,
With peaceful wings unfurled;
And still their heav'nly music floats
O'er all the weary world:
Above its sad and lowly plains
They bend on hov'ring wing;
And ever o'er its Babel-sounds
The blessèd angels sing.

3 Yet with the woes of sin and strife
The world has suffered long;
Beneath the angel-strain have rolled
Two-thousand years of wrong;
And warring humankind hears not
The love-song which they bring:
O hush the noise of mortal strife,
And hear the angels sing!

4 And ye, beneath life's crushing load,
Whose forms are bending low,
Who toil along the climbing way
With painful steps and slow:
Look now! For glad and golden hours
Come swiftly on the wing;
O rest beside the weary road,
And hear the angels sing.

5 For lo, the days are hast'ning on,
By prophets seen of old,
When with the ever-circling years
Comes 'round the age of gold;
When peace shall over all the earth
Its ancient splendors fling,
And all the world give back the song
Which now the angels sing.

Good Christian Men, Rejoice

Words by J.M. Neale
Music: Traditional

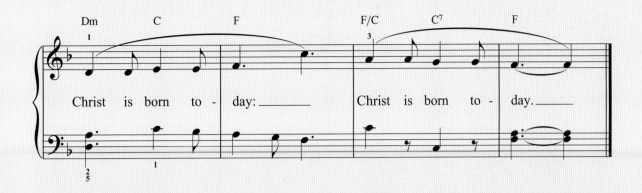

Christ is born to - day: _____ Christ is born to - day. _____

2 Good Christian men, rejoice
With heart, and soul, and voice;
Now ye hear of endless bliss:
Joy! Joy!
Jesus Christ was born for this!
He has opened the heavenly door,
And man is blessed forevermore.
Christ was born for this!
Christ was born for this!

3 Good Christian men, rejoice
With heart, and soul, and voice;
Now ye need not fear the grave:
Peace! Peace!
Jesus Christ was born to save;
Calls you one and calls you all,
To gain His everlasting hall.
Christ was born to save!
Christ was born to save!

God Rest Ye Merry, Gentlemen

Traditional

Steadily, not too fast

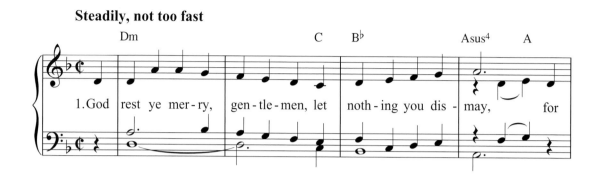

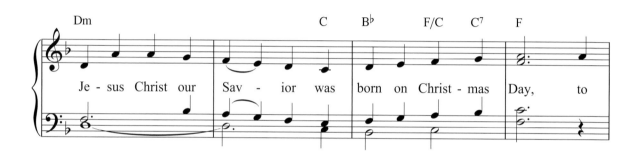

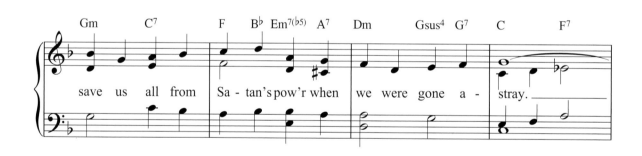

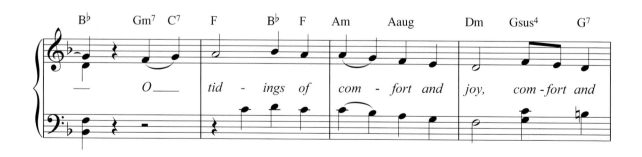

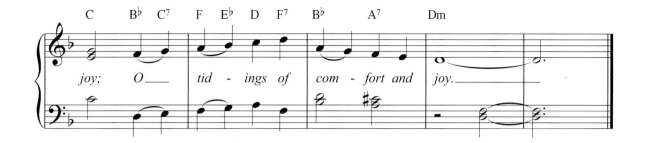

joy; O___ tid - ings of com - fort and joy.___

2 In Bethlehem, in Jewry,
This blessèd babe was born,
And laid within a manger,
Upon this blessèd morn;
The which his mother Mary
Did nothing take in scorn.

O tidings of comfort and joy…

3 From God, our heav'nly Father,
A blessèd angel came,
And unto certain shepherds
Brought tidings of the same
How that in Bethlehem was born
The Son of God by name.

O tidings of comfort and joy…

4 "Fear not," then said the angel,
"Let nothing you affright,
This day is born a Savior,
Of virtue, pow'r and might;
By Him the world is overcome
And Satan put to flight."

O tidings of comfort and joy…

5 The shepherds at those tidings
Rejoicèd much in mind,
And left their flocks a-feeding,
In tempest, storm and wind,
And went to Bethlehem straightway
This blessèd babe to find.

O tidings of comfort and joy…

6 But when to Bethlehem they came,
Whereat this infant lay,
They found him in a manger,
Where oxen feed on hay;
His mother Mary kneeling,
Unto the Lord did pray.

O tidings of comfort and joy…

7 Now to the Lord sing praises,
All you within this place,
And with true love and fellowship
Each other now embrace;
This holy tide of Christmas
All others doth deface.

O tidings of comfort and joy…

Says Simeon:

Glory be to God! Let all my longings cease...

Now I've seen your salvation, And I can go in peace.

And Anna lifts her hands—

Dear God... the good things which you gave, Are nothing when compared to this; A child who's born to save!

Now God was pleased
with what He'd done,
And so He thought
He'd try
To bring others
to see the baby,
So He hung a star
up in the sky.

Some clever men who watched the skies
From across the hills so far...

47

They found the baby there...

And worshipped him, and gave him gifts—
Gold, frankincense and myrrh.

The First Noel

Traditional

Moderately

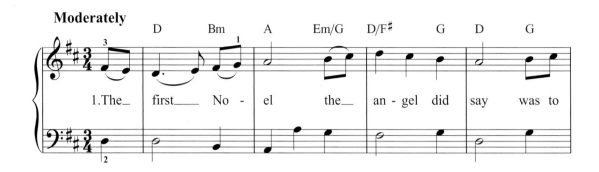

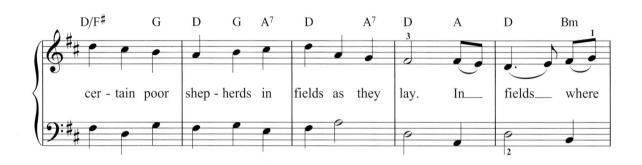

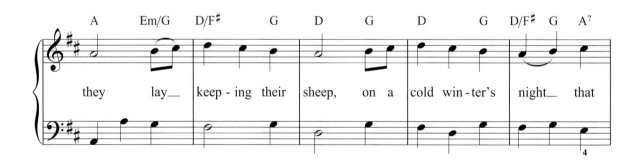

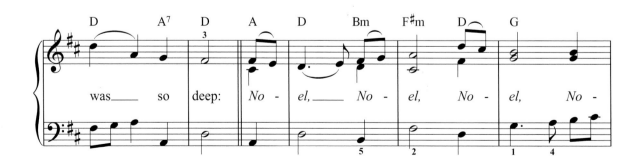

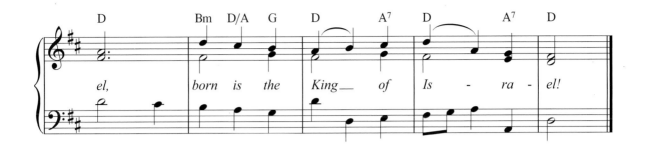

el,   *born is the King___ of Is - ra - el!*

2 They lookèd up and saw a star,
Shining in the east, beyond them far,
And to the earth it gave great light,
And so it continued both day and night.

Noel, Noel...

3 And by the light of that same star,
Three wise men came from country far;
To seek for a King was their intent,
And to follow the star wherever it went.

Noel, Noel...

4 This star drew nigh to the north-west,
O'er Bethlehem it took its rest,
And there it did both stop and stay
Right over the place where Jesus lay.

Noel, Noel...

5 Then entered in those wise men three,
Full rev'rently upon their knee,
And offered there in his presence,
Their gold and myrrh and frankincense.

Noel, Noel...

6 Then let us all with one accord
Sing praises to our heav'nly Lord,
That hath made heav'n and earth of naught,
And with his blood mankind hath bought.

Noel, Noel...

As With Gladness Men Of Old

Words by William Chatterton Dix
Music by Conrad Kocher

2 As with joyful steps they sped
To that lowly manger bed,
There to bend the knee before
Him who heav'n and earth adore,
So may we with willing feet
Ever seek Thy mercy seat.

3 As their precious gifts they laid,
At thy manger roughly made,
So may we with holy joy,
Pure, and free from sin's alloy,
All our costliest treasures bring,
Christ, to thee, our heav'nly King.

4 Holy Jesus, ev'ry day
Keep us in the narrow way;
And, when earthly things are past,
Bring our ransomed souls at last
Where they need no star to guide,
Where no clouds thy glory hide.

5 In the heav'nly country bright
Need they no created light;
Thou its light, its joy, its crown,
Thou its sun which goes not down;
There for ever may we sing
Alleluias to our King.

We Three Kings Of Orient Are

Words & Music by John Henry Hopkins

Smooth and flowing

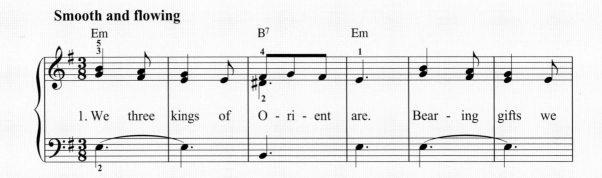

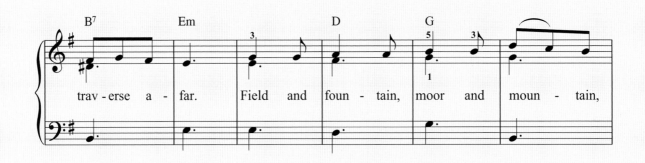

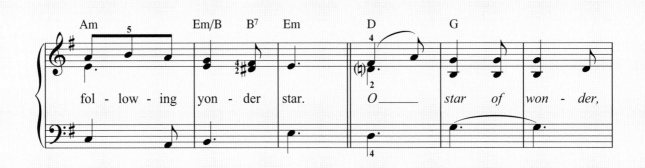

lead - ing, still pro - ceed - ing, guide us to thy per - fect light.

2 Born a King on Bethlehem plain,
Gold I bring, to crown him again,
King forever, ceasing never,
Over us all to reign.

O star of wonder, star of night...

3 Frankincense to offer have I,
Incense owns a Deity nigh,
Prayer and praising, gladly raising,
Worship him, God most high.

O star of wonder, star of night...

4 Myrrh is mine, its bitter perfume
Breathes a life of gathering gloom;
Sorrowing, sighing, bleeding, dying,
Sealed in the stone-cold tomb.

O star of wonder, star of night...

5 Glorious now behold him arise,
King and God and sacrifice;
Alleluia, alleluia,
Earth to heav'n replies.

O star of wonder, star of night...

Behold That Star

Traditional African-American Spiritual

Moderate

Be - hold that star,____ be - hold that

star up yon - der. Be - hold that star,____

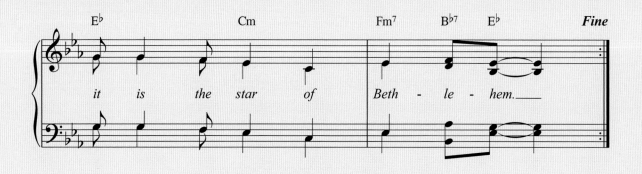

it is the star of Beth - le - hem.____ *Fine*

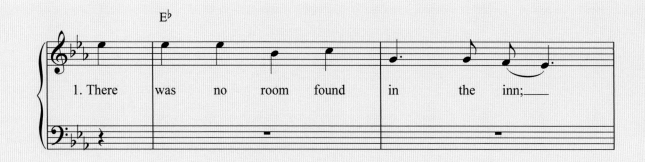

1. There was no room found in the inn;____

It is the star of Beth - le - hem.___ For

Him who was born___ free from sin;___

It is the star of Beth - le - hem.___ O

2 The wise men traveled from the East,
It is the star of Bethlehem.
To worship Him, the Prince of Peace.
It is the star of Bethlehem.

O behold that star...

3 A song broke forth upon the night,
It is the star of Bethlehem.
From angel hosts all robed in white.
It is the star of Bethlehem.

O behold that star...

58

The angel came again, to Joseph...

King Herod has a plan... Quick! Pack up your belongings! Escape this dreadful man!

For Christ had come at Christmas, Such important work to do...

That God protected his own Son As he through childhood grew...

Into a man with God's own heart,
His one desire to help the poor,
The sick and blind, the weak and lame,
And then he died and rose once more.

And here's the greatest news of all—
We sing because it's true;
Jesus came for you and me
Because he loves US, too!

Joy To The World!

Words by Isaac Watts
Music by George Frideric Handel

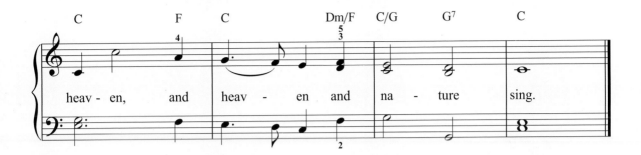

heav - en,   and   heav - en and   na - ture   sing.

2 Joy to the earth! The Savior reigns;
Let us our songs employ;
While fields and floods, rocks, hills and plains
Repeat the sounding joy,
Repeat the sounding joy,
Repeat, repeat the sounding joy.

3 He rules the world with truth and grace,
And makes the nations prove
The glories of his righteousness,
And wonders of his love,
And wonders of his love,
And wonders, and wonders of his love.

O Come, All Ye Faithful

Words & Music by John Francis Wade

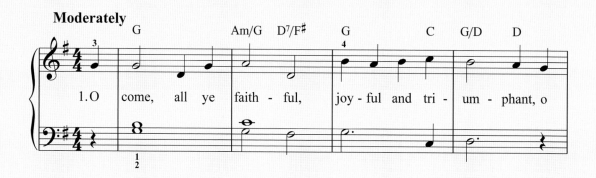

1.O come, all ye faith - ful, joy - ful and tri - um - phant, o

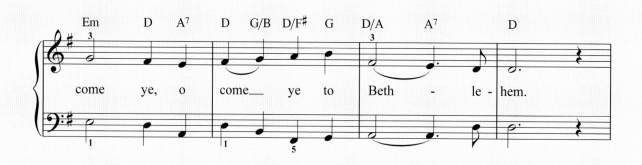

come ye, o come__ ye to Beth - le - hem.

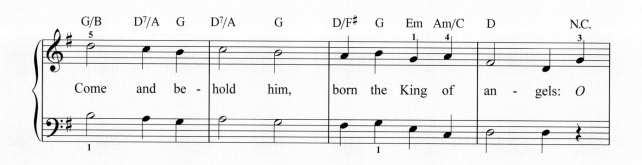

Come and be - hold him, born the King of an - gels: O

come, let us a - dore him, o come, let us a - dore him, o

come, let us a - dore him,___ Christ___ the Lord.

2 God of God,
Light of light,
Lo! He abhors not the Virgin's womb;
Very God, begotten, not created:

O come, let us adore him...

3 Sing choirs of angels,
Sing in exultation,
Sing all ye citizens of heav'n above;
Glory to God in the highest:

O come, let us adore him...

4 Yea, Lord, we greet thee,
Born this happy morning,
Jesu, to thee be glory giv'n;
Word of the Father, now in flesh appearing:

O come, let us adore him...

Hark! The Herald Angels Sing

Words by Charles Wesley
Music by Felix Mendelssohn

Moderately

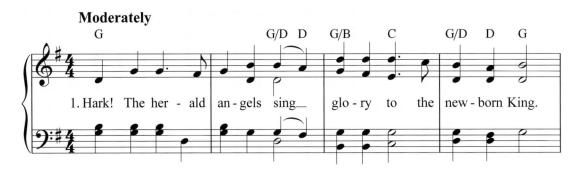

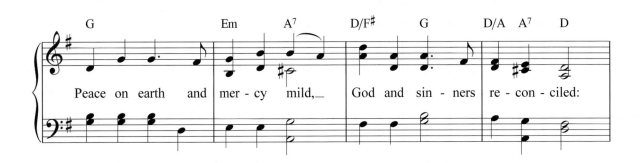

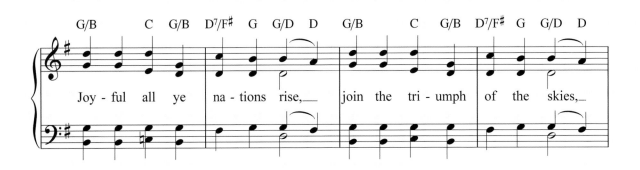

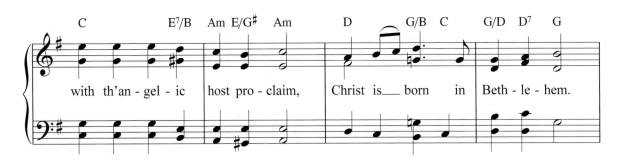

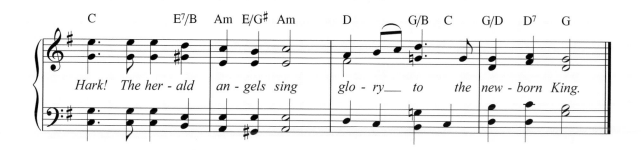

2 Christ, by highest heav'n adored,
Christ, the everlasting Lord,
Late in time behold him come,
Offspring of a Virgin's womb!
Veiled in flesh the Godhead see,
Hail, the incarnate Deity!
Pleased as man with us to dwell,
Jesus, our Emmanuel.

Hark! The herald angels sing...

3 Hail, the heav'n-born Prince of Peace!
Hail, the Son of Righteousness!
Light and life to all he brings,
Ris'n with healing in his wings;
Mild he lays His glory by,
Born that we no more may die,
Born to raise us from the earth,
Born to give us second birth.

Hark! The herald angels sing...

Go Tell It On The Mountain

Traditional

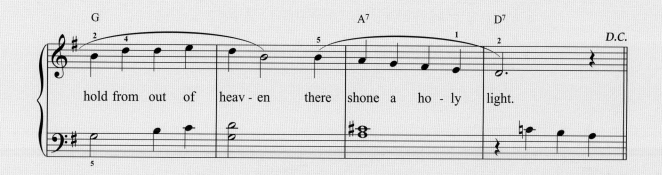

hold from out of heav - en there shone a ho - ly light.

2 The shepherds feared and trembled,
When lo! Above the earth
Rang out the angel chorus
That hailed our Jesus' birth.

Go, tell it on the mountain...

3 And lo! When they had heard it
They all bowed down to pray;
Then traveled on together
To where the baby lay.

Go, tell it on the mountain...

4 Down in a lowly manger
The humble babe was born;
And God sent down his angels
That blessed Christmas morn.

Go, tell it on the mountain...

Ding Dong! Merrily On High

Words by George Woodward
Music: Traditional

- - - - ri - a, ho - san - na in ex - cel - sis.

2 E'en so here below, below,
Let steeple bells be swungen,
And i-o, i-o, i-o,
By priest and people sungen.

Gloria, hosanna in excelsis...

3 Pray you, dutifully prime
Your matin chime, ye ringers;
May you beautifully rhyme
Your evetime song, ye singers.

Gloria, hosanna in excelsis...